Table of Contents

Incipient thoughts

What if you could achieve your own life of freedom by encompassing everything you thought was a prerequisite?

Can you develop a significant life oriented toward something you love to do?

If one of your goals is to become a millionaire, you have to learn to think the way millionaires think and get the results, especially financial results, a millionaire gets.

The most important attitudes for financial success are called long-term thinking and visualization.

Successful people think a long way into the future and they adjust their daily behavior to ensure they achieve long-term goals.

Another key attitude that matters in getting results is time perspective. This is a great breakthrough made by financial scientists.

Time perspective refers to the amount of time you take into consideration when planning your daily activities and making substantial decisions in your life.

People with long-term perspectives invariably move up economically in the course of their lifetimes.

When you spend weeks, months, and years developing your skills and abilities, expanding your experience to be successful, then you have a long-time perspective. Self-development plays a fundamental role in moulding the character and perspective.

This book is about becoming a self-made millionaire.

The starting point of becoming a millionaire is to remember the greatest discovery of all human life, which is that *"You become what you think about most of the time."*

If you sincerely want to be rich, to achieve all your financial goals, one of the smartest things you can do is to develop habits of thinking and acting that enable others to become self-made millionaires.

Most people are thinking of how little money they have, they worry about being broke, about poverty, and they are wondering why they are not flourishing financially.

Because they are thinking about poverty and lack rather that prosperity and abundance.

Some people see the glass half-empty, whereas others see it half-full. This is the antagonism between perspectives, which is influenced by optimism or pessimism.

Optimists see the glass half-full and they are more likely to succeed whereas pessimists see the glass half-empty. They have reduced chances to achieve their goals because of the way they perceive life. But even pessimists can change their life through changing their character and vision.

This book is about reinventing the way you live your life. It is about designing financial goals and working toward accomplishing them.

It is about major ways of becoming a millionaire using knowledge, experience, and determination to bring abundance into your life.

Reinvent the way you live, do what you love and what represents you the most, then create a new future!

Imagine a life where you do what you want, when you want, with whom you want, where you want...this is freedom.

Imagine telling to your boss while packing your stuff, *"Boss, I don't need your services anymore. Thanks for everything, but I'll be doing things my own way from now on."*

Imagine that today is your final day of working in that bondage machine that creates prototypes closed in involution circles.

What if, very soon, not so far from today, you will be ready to work by using a laptop in your home office, doing what you want instead of what someone tells you to do?

In this tremendous world, in many different ways, thousands of people have chosen to do exactly the same thing as you.

They rewrite the rules of work, choosing to design a new future, a future that is under the auspices of their mind: they become their own bosses.

The old principles no longer work in the new economy. Businesses have reached the old model's limits with respect to complexity and speed.

Great shifts, genuine and radical transformations have defined the economy and business in recent decades.

Technology, information and communication, has changed the requirements of the business environment, facilitating growth and changing the dynamics of development, breaking the boundaries of rusty principles.

It is a microbusiness revolution, a manner of earning a decent or exceptional living while crafting a life of independence and purpose.

This new model of doing business is based on two themes: *freedom* and *value*.

Freedom represents the thing we crave while value is the way of achieving it. Every destination has a direction, no?

This is why I have developed a career as a writer. I have combined passion with the desire of achieving financial freedom. I'm doing the things I have learned from every business: start with an idea, then figure out things along the way. This was my own way of rewriting the old rules of success. The path to freedom.

The second thing I had to do was to create value. The value is created when a person makes something useful and shares it with the entire world.

The value comes from the action you take on something you love to do: a passion, a skill, or a hobby that turns into a business model. This is the impetus of freedom.

If you are tired to work for someone else's dreams, and if you are tired of working 8 hours a day without having a satisfaction of taking a vacation that you deserve, the solution is here.

The solution is you and the way you perceive your life. Working for someone else means you trade the scarcest resource you have for money — *TIME*.

The problem is that you don't realize that time is more valuable than money, it is priceless, but you have decided to sell it very cheap for someone else's goals instead of using it for your purposes and objectives.

This is the worst deal you can make.

The secret of success is to value your time more than anything.

Don't wait so long for a raise, learn to work for yourself and pay yourself first. Don't work for money, let money work for you.

Passive income can be thought of as money you earn passively, meaning that it only requires a little bit of effort on your part to earn that revenue. From my experience, I have learned that achieving success takes time, commitment to excellence, and a significant drop of patience. But you can't imagine the feeling of succeeding. Making essential steps for your success and getting results is the most significant motivator. Nothing motivates you more than getting results.

It gives you power, and it gives you strength to resist to downturns and expect for consistent returns in the future. It makes you wise.

The benefits of this business model are enormous:

1. Flexible schedule: You decide how much you work for achieving your goals and you can have however many free days you want.

2. More time for your personal plan: Imagine yourself working while travelling by train or laying on the beach with a laptop on a table in the Bahamas while contemplating the marvelous view of the ocean, checking your emails, money, and stats.

3. Less stress: No one tells you what to do or how much to work. You can take as many breaks as you want.

4. Fast Growth: If you work full-time for a company, you will grow, you will get higher wages if you work efficiently, you will be promoted, but this happens in a matter of months or even years. Passive income will bring you more time than you have ever dreamed.

5. You invest in yourself: It may be the most profitable investment you will ever make. It will increase the quality of your life and future. You will develop new skills, explore your creativity, and nurture your body and mind. Investing in yourself truly makes a difference in your life, your well-being, and your ability to thrive and perform to the best of your ability. The extent to which you invest in yourself, mind and body, not only shapes the way you interact with the outside world, but it also often reflects the opinion you have of yourself. Your future is in large part determined by your willingness and ability to invest in yourself now.

6. You can hire other people easily: You can hire people to do simple tasks or time-consuming tasks to grow your income and business faster. Some simple but time-consuming tasks may negatively affect your performance. And the best part is that you can hire freelancers inexpensively, without contracts or much effort. It's simple, you hire the best people you find and the ones who work hard and effectively.

Passive income is money made from stock dividends, properties rental, interest on notes, affiliate marketing, social trading, money lending, and so on. The truth is that you can't achieve passive income without working for it. Every investment requires some sort of work.

Chapter 1: Find Your Financial Position and Define Your Financial Freedom Plan

Before starting your long journey on this path called freedom, you have to know your financial situation in this moment. You might have assets such as buildings or land that could earn you passive income but they don't, just because you didn't take action.

The ideal method is to create a list on a piece of paper or open an excel sheet in which you put down all the assets you have and try to estimate their value: house, car, businesses, cards, stocks, and much more.

Now that you have identified your assets, let's think about their value.

In your list, you have assets that can bring money and others that consume money.

A clear example is the car that consumes money for its maintenance.

You need to pay for fuel, taxes, insurance, and for car parts if it breaks. So your car is a big expenditure source. But if you have a rental car service, you will lend it and this turns into service delivery that will generate income. You converted this asset into a money resource.

Try to apply this analogy to all your properties. If you rent them to someone, they will become a source of passive income. If you don't, you will pay taxes on the property and also pay for maintenance. You have to explore every possibility and try to see the benefits of them.

Now write down all your liabilities. The liabilities are obligations arising from the past transactions or events, the settlement of which may result in the transfer or use of assets, provision of services, or other yielding of economic benefits in the future (loans, credits, or mortgages).

The next step is to write down all your expenses and income sources for the month coming from the assets and liabilities you have.

The expenses come from liabilities such as mortgage payments and the passive income comes from assets (dividend stock).

For your expenses, write the taxes, rents, mortgage payments, loan payments, and maintenance costs of the car in a column. In another column, put down the income sources such as salary, interests, and dividends.

After this, you have to subtract the expenses from your incomes and you will get your monthly net income.

Chapter 2: The Main Pillars of Financial Freedom

If there is a common goal we share in this world, and that is making money and improving our personal finance.

However, only a small percentage of us achieve this goal. The reasons are determination and action. One without the other can't exist.

The good news is that, today, you can get financial freedom faster than ever before. Proper financial planning and specific goals will bring you in the millionaires' zone.

Here is a seven point formula that you can use to achieve money and financial freedom. It is based on increasing the productivity performance and output by one half of 1% per week. This one half percent improvement can be achieved with suitable prioritization of your tasks each day. By improving these key elements of development, success will be closer than ever before.

1. The Golden Hour

Every morning, two hours before starting work, invest the first hour in yourself. This is called *"The Golden Hour"*. You will leverage your potential and productivity. It sets the tone for everything that happens afterward. If you read one hour each morning, this will become one book per week, which means that you work on your personal development.

This will translate into about 50 books per year, 500 books over the next ten years. Your performance and output will be increased consistently and significantly.

"Once you stop learning, you start dying."-Albert Einstein

2. Rewrite your major goals for financial freedom

Set your short- and long-term goals, rewrite and review them every day, and think about an action program/action plan for accomplishing them. This will take you between five and ten minutes. Thinking about your goals will increase your productivity and desire to achieve them by one half percent per week, 2% per month, 24% per year.

"Ask yourself if what you are doing today is getting you closer to where you want to be tomorrow."

3. Plan every day in advance.

The best moment to set the action plan for every day is the night before. This will make you sharper and more precise with your plans. You will achieve better focus, higher sense of self-control, and personal power when you work on your plans. The level of efficiency will increase with 25 the first day.

4. The principle of concentration

Try to focus your concentration on the most important task every hour of every day. Try to find the most valuable use of time. This principle of concentration will bring you closer to your financial freedom. This habit of concentration will do more to ensure your personal finance success than any other skill or habit you can acquire.

"Concentration is the root of all the higher abilities in man."

5. Listen to audio programs to make more money

Listen to audio programs whenever you can: at home, in the car, or in a coffee shop in the morning. This will turn you into one of the most knowledgeable and the most skilled people in your field.

It is well-known that we spend 500 to 1,000 hours per year behind the wheel, so you should turn your car into a university on wheels. It will give you an increase of one half per week and more over time.

"Small daily improvements are the key to staggering long-term results."

6. Magic questions

At every important event in your life, ask yourself the two "Magic questions": "What did I do right?" and "What could I do differently next time?" By reviewing your performance after every event, presentation, or meeting, you will increase your efficiency by understanding what holds you back and what moves you forward.

The advantage of these questions is that the answers are every time positive. You will tend to even better the next time. To double or triple your speed of learning and improving your performance, you should write down everything you did and what you would do differently.

"My life is constantly under construction. There's always something to improve."

7. Learn to appreciate

The last point is to treat everyone you meet like a million dollar customer. Treating people as the most important person in your life, while they have the opinion (because everyone believes that he or she is the most important in the world), they will give you recognition and acknowledge more than you can imagine.

"Appreciation can make a day, even change a life. Your willingness to put it into words is all that is necessary."

Chapter 3: Pay yourself first

One of the oldest rules of personal finance is to pay yourself first. It is not about taking a percentage of your money and spend it in the town with friends or family, it is about saving money to invest.

Before you pay your bills, before you buy groceries, before you do anything else, set aside a portion of your income to save. The first bill you pay each month should be to yourself. This habit, developed early, can help you build an outstanding wealth.

Why pay yourself first?

In the real world, this habit seems to be impossible to be followed. Sure, you would like to save money, but at the end of the month, there is no money left because you maybe have rent, a loan, or you have to buy groceries. The big problem is that most people save what's left over after bills and discretionary spending. There will always be a reason to delay the development of this habit, that's why you should start with it first.

Here are three reasons you should start saving money instead of waiting until next year:

1. When you pay yourself first, you are mentally establishing saving as a priority. You are telling yourself that you are more important than the car company or the bank. Building this habit brings you motivation, it empowers you.

2. Paying yourself first encourages sound financial habits. The current situation is that most people spend their money in this order: bills, fun, saving. Most of the time, they realize that there's no money left for saving. But if you bring saving in the front, so that it is saving, bills, then fun, you will be able to reserve money before you rationalize reasons to spend it.

#3. By paying yourself first, you are building a cash buffer with real-world applications. Paying yourself first gives you freedom. It opens a world of great opportunities. You can use the money to deal with emergencies, buy a house, or save for retirement.

How to Pay Yourself First

The most efficient way to develop a saving habit is to make it as painless as possible. This means that the process should be automatic and invisible. You should arrange to save money before receiving the paycheck, this way, you will never feel its absence. The main reason of saving should be the accomplishment of your long-term goals, not retirement.

> *1. Open a high interest savings account at a bank like Capital One 360 or FNBO Direct.* Set up the automatic transfers into this account, either directly from your paycheck or from your regular

account. You should treat these transfers like regular obligations to the bank. Your future is the most important bill you should pay every month.

#2. Start a Roth IRA (Individual Retirement Arrangement). These accounts allow your investments to grow tax-free. Because of the extraordinary potential of compound interest and returns, regular investments represent a key to future wealth.

#3. If your employer provides a retirement plan such as a 401(k), you should enroll as soon as possible. Only if you haven't decided yet to hire yourself.

The real impediment to developing this pattern is finding money to save. Most of us think it's impossible. But let me tell you that everyone can save at least 1% of their income. If a skeptic will try to save only 1% of his income in the first month, he will discover that this is painless, and next month, he will definitely save 3%-5%.

No matter what your age is, you should try to develop this habit. It is the first step to financial security and freedom that will drive you to a bright future.

Your goal should be to build or buy assets that can generate passive income. This is the only reason you should save money. Don't fail in the trap of saving money for a long-term goal without investing it. If you don't invest it, you will never have the joy of letting it to work for you. You will keep working for it.

Chapter 4. Lending Money Online

Lending money via Social Lending Networks

With the United States' economy flirting with the word "recession", people were looking to get out of debt.

Banks were not always willing to give out loans to paying off a credit card and this situation led to social lending.

The core values of these platforms are the speed and efficiency through technology and the ability to service borrowers at speeds banks never could. They met needs that banks couldn't or wouldn't. They provide lower interest rates for borrowers and higher returns that they would receive by parking their money in a savings account.

The peer-to-peer lending appeared as a solution to the necessity of covering debts.

The lending takes place online on peer-to-peer lending companies' websites, using various lending platforms and credit checking tools.

The interest rates are set by lenders who compete for the lowest rate on the reverse auction model or are fixed by the intermediary company on the basis of an analysis of the borrower's credit.

Peer-to-Peer Lending Sources:

1. Lending Club - Lenders and borrowers find something in common

2. Prosper.com - The original eBay for loans

3. Zopa.com
4 . Funding Circle

Lending Club:

People interested in a way to safely invest their extra cash considered the platform, Lending Club, as a tremendous opportunity to earn money passively.

Since it was launched in 2007, the peer-to-peer lender has paid over $540 million to thousands of investors, with most of them earning a 5-9% return per year.

This company continues to experience over 100% annual growth and it's regularly mentioned in one of the most promising company in America specialized in news, Forbes.

How it Works

The company uses the Internet to connect people who need a loan with people who want to invest their money to obtain passive income by lending them.

This program of lending is called peer-to-peer lending and it is a revolutionary way of thinking about finances, especially in America. It is a loan without the frustrating intervention of banks. The main advantage is the low interest rate provided to the borrowers.

As an investor, you get a return by lending your money to the creditworthy borrowers. You achieve the money by investing in notes or $25 portions each loan. This way, you can extend your investment across hundreds of loans, while the borrowers can have loans funded by hundreds of different investors.

This system is called "the crowdfunding of loans over the Internet".

There are 3 steps of peer-to-peer lending:

1. You open your account and invest in notes, which are portions of loans.
2. Borrowers pay their loans back month by month and you receive the interest.
3. You take those payments and you can invest more, growing your account.

Reasons you should do this:

1. Return of 5-10% per year

This is the main reason why people invest their savings using this platform. The loans they fund have a 14% interest rate. They have to reduce a 4-5% default rate, plus 1% given to Lending Club in fees and they totally receive 8% return. (14%-6%=8%)

2. A substantial investment

The reason the peer-to-peer loans are tremendous investments is because this type of loans is less laced to the stock market than traditional investments. This is why, in the recession in 2008, when the national economy faced the worst financial fall since the Great Depression (1929-1933), the Lending Club managed to return investors 3% overall.

3. Peer-to-peer lending just makes sense

Think about your contribution to society. Think about how your money can help people who really need help in critical situations. You can help them to get rid of debt.

Investing through this platform does involve risk:

4. Risk - Defaulting loans is the most common

A default loan is a loan that a borrower has failed to pay back. These are "unsecured" debts because they are not guaranteed by a house or any sort of collateral. If you invest your money and your borrowers want to declare bankruptcy, you will lose all the money you had invested.

To repel this, you should diversify your investment. Spread your investment across at least 2,000 loans. It will keep your default rate at a small and reasonable level.

5. Risk - Rising interest rates is less likely

A rise in the national rate can affect Lending Club's business level. Investors can get a risk-free 6% return in the saving account and they don't have to struggle to earn this 6% with borrowers who might default on their loans. The platform might fight to find investors with lower-risk loans who earn 5-6%, but there would still be demand for medium-risk loans that return 7-10%.

6. Risk - Lending Club may go bankrupt, which is unlikely

In this case, a backup servicer would work to funnel borrower payments to investors. It has never happened before, so they don't expect it because the Lending Club is experiencing a phenomenal success.

Now that you know the risks of this kind of investment, you should also know that the most important thing that will bring you success in this process is diversification.

The reason new investors fail is because they don't diversify their loans enough. If you want to invest in this business, you should spread your cash across 200+ equally-weighted notes. The minimum amount (loan portion) is $25 so you should start with $5,000 (200*$25=5,000).

How to Invest on Lending Club:

Go to http://www.lendingclub.com/ , sign in there and transfer funds, create a portfolio by investing in a range of loans in increments as little as $25. Receive monthly payments of principal and interest as borrowers repay their loans.

Reinvest payments or withdraw. This should be your process there.

Here is the main account page:

- The account's return: 13,44%
- Current value: $18,543.70
- Earned interest: $4,666.66

Here are the most important indicators of the investment.

The list of loans is available in the Browse Notes. Each of these loans represents a borrower who passed the credit standards established by the Lending Club.

You can sort and filter the list of notes by different criteria to find the appropriate investment for you.

The Lending Club has 7 loan grades (A is the safest and G is the riskiest one) measuring the loan's risk. This is one of the most important factors of an investment. You can find it in the Rate column. A is colored with blue and G with orange.

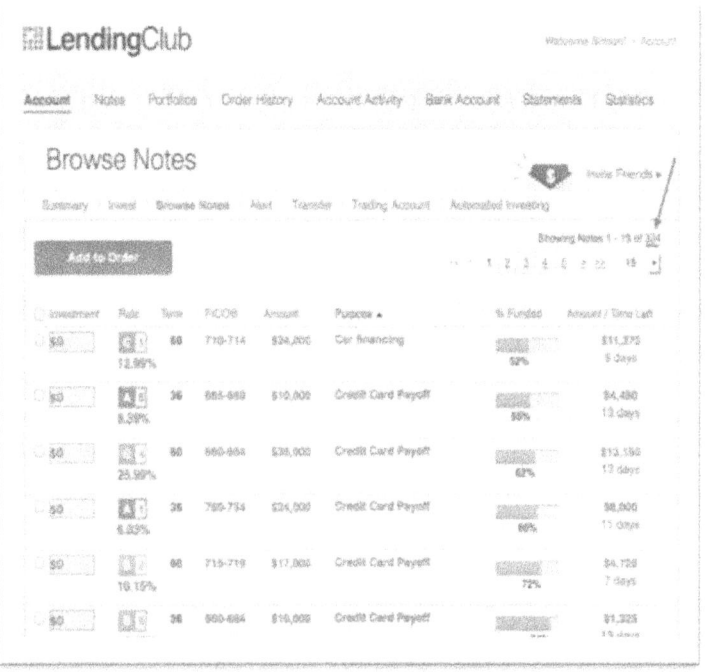

Investing Became Easier with the Automated Investing Tool.

If you want to use it, you have to select the ideal mix of loan grades (risk) and note size ($25) then, set the tool to invest in loans automatically for you.

You choose the type of investment that represents you the most. After this, you will receive daily emails telling you that Lending Club invested in notes that meet your criteria. The process becomes so easy with this tool.

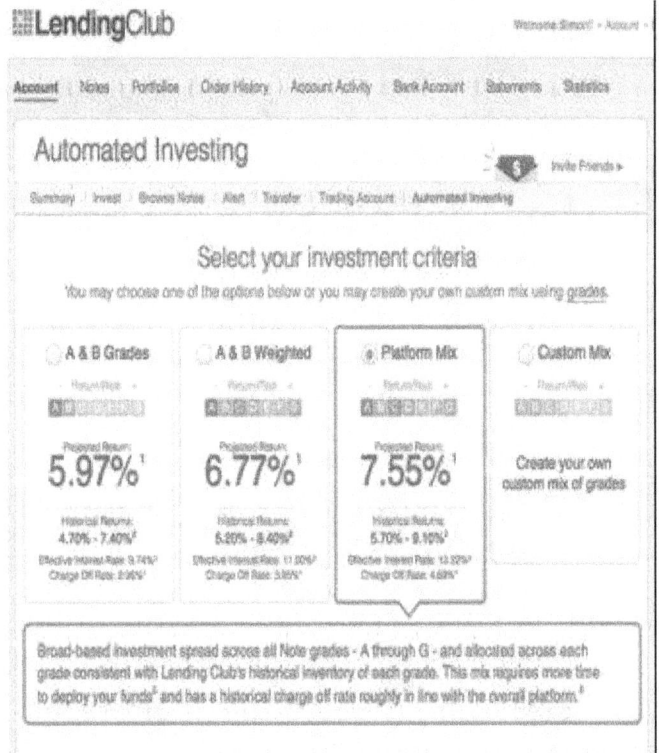

How to Choose the Risk Tolerance:

There are different degrees of risk you can assume as a Lending Club investor. If you want to choose the safest method, you should invest in just A and B-grade loans. Or you can choose the model of successful investors: they spread their investment across all the different loan grades to achieve a balance of risk and return. Remember what I've told you: Diversification.

For an A-grade loan, borrowers pay only 6%. After defaults, you will earn around 5% on these loans. But if you invest in riskier loans like D-grades, you will receive 8-10% of the loans after reducing the defaults and fees because borrowers pay 17-20% on these loans.

Lending Club
Loan Grades

A	6-9%
B	10-14%
C	14-17%
D	17-20%
E	21-22.5%
F	23-24%
G	25%

Current 5/2/13

If you're considering starting a business, peer-to-peer lending is a concrete option that involves real people who choose to invest in someone else's dreams, visions, or needs.

It may seem to be a risky business and it is, but it depends on your investment strategy. Choosing the best strategy will guarantee you huge profit.

Chapter 5: Building a Blog for Passive Income

How in the world does a blog make you passive income?

Simple. **Traffic.**

The more people you bring to your website, the higher the potential for those visitors to click on an ad and buy a product/service.

Advertisers know this and depending on the theme of your site and what it can do for them, they will be willing to pay to work with you. This comes either in the form of direct advertising or affiliate marketing.

The secret to be successful as a blogger is to find an interesting theme, draw an audience, and keep them committed by using an email list, sending them email where they can benefits from information or promotions.

How to Start a Blog and Make Money from it:

If you want to start a career as an entrepreneur, blogging might be an overwhelming path for financial freedom.

Let me introduce you into the journey:

1. What do you want your blog to be about?

This is the first question you should ask yourself before writing any post or coming up with a name for your blog.

The key to success is to choose a topic you are really passionate about because if you don't, it will be very hard to run your blog and your potential to make money will decrease as well.

You need to convince your audience that what you do and write there comes from passion and enthusiasm, not from your ferocious desire to make money.

What interests you?

If a stranger would come to you and start a conversation, what topic do you feel like the two of you could talk about for hours and hours on end?

This is exactly what it will be like if you start your blog. You should be able to write at least 50 distinct articles on your selected topic. This is the winning topic for your blog, the one that communicates great ideas without having an end.

What do you want your niche to be?

The blogs that are more specific on a subject or problem tend bring more money than the diverse ones.

Why?

- Because readers are looking for specific answers in the content of your article.
- If readers find a correlation between articles, they will read more.

- Search engines like them more because they see them as a better fit and will direct more organic traffic to them.

Readers find the ads more useful and they tend to click on them more often.

What can the readers expect from your blog?

- *To solve problems*
- *To learn something*
- *To satisfy their curiosity*
- *To be entertained*

If your blog doesn't satisfy one of the basic needs of the reader, he won't come back on your site. This means that your traffic lowers and there's no chance of making any money.

2. Finding a web host and a domain name

WordPress is a free, but the personal domain name (YourSiteName.com) and hosting (service that connects your site with the Internet) will cost you. If you don't get hosting or a domain name, your site will look unprofessional.

I would suggest www.iPage.com as a domain name and hosting register.

Their hosting package is one of the cheapest, less than $2 per month with a free domain name included. They have "one-click-install" for WordPress, Drupal, and Joomia platforms, so you don't need to set up your site manually.

When you choose your possible domain name, think about these three characteristics of a successful blog name: brandable, memorable, and catchy.

3. Setting up your WordPress website

Firstly, you need to install WordPress to your domain. You need to sign up with iPage or any other hosting company and you can use "one-click-installation" in your account control panel.

- *Log in to your hosting account.*

- *Go to your control panel.*
- *Look for the "WordPress" icon.*
- *Choose the domain where you want to install your website.*
- *Click "Install Now" button and you will access your new WordPress website.*

4. Choose the right theme or layout for your website.

You need to choose a theme that fits the overall topic of your website. Some of them are free, but you have to pay if you want something professional on ThemeForest.net.

5. Add content and create new pages

Once you have chosen the theme, you can start creating content.

To create pages like "About" or "Resources", you need to head over the WordPress dashboard and find "Pages" – "Add New". To make them appear on the menu as well, you have to go to "Appearance"- "Menus" and add them on the list.

6. Install plugins to get the most out of your website

These plugins will add value to your website and will make it unique.

To install plugins, go *to* "Plugins" –"Add New" and you will find over 25,000 different free plugins.

Now you have your own website!

Now comes the most interesting part: making money with your blog.

There are so many ways to make an income from running a website, but I will discuss the most important tools.

Google AdSense is a free affiliate program from Google where you put some codes on your site in certain places to create dynamic advertisements.

These advertisements change depending on who the visitor to the site is. The display works with the reader's cookies and it is made to target ads from the niche audience (your niche).

They can generate revenue on either a per-click or per-impression basis.

Amazon Associates is the second most popular affiliate program on the Internet.

You place links to products that Amazon sells on your website. Every time someone clicks on one of the links to buy the product, you are paid a commission.

This service is free and you get paid sustainably. Another advantage is that even if a person buys other product than the one you are promoting, you still get paid.

This strategy can bring you over a thousand dollars per month.

Other Affiliate Programs. The mechanism is the same. You get paid for promoting certain products and services on your site.

ClickBank is another affiliate program that will bring the success to your blog. It promotes very specific products (software, e-books, etc.).

Direct advertising is a strategy that will definitely bring you money. Sometimes, people come to you and ask you to promote their products on your website. This is happening when you have traffic and your blog is very visible on the Internet. It is your job to make it visible and drive quality traffic. Remember that traffic leads to the monetization of these advertising strategies.

Ads without traffic mean nothing.

Direct advertising is based on posts, reviews, blog mentions, and even banners with the product on your website. What is more important, you will be paid no matter how the advertisement goes.

Chapter 6. Investing in Social Trading

Social trading has been seen as one of the most significant shifts in trading because of its potential to open up outstanding opportunities for those interested in stock markets. It is one of the biggest growth areas when it comes to trading.

Online financial investors rely on the financial content collected from different Internet applications as a decisive source of information for making financial trading decisions.

They can use investment social indicators in their decision process, which can be found in social financial analysis, fueled by a transparent, real-time trading data-feed of all users from the social trading network.

It is very popular in currency and commodity investing.

It allows individuals to follow a successful member of a given platform in and out of specific trades. If you see someone who is expert in Euro/Dollar transactions, you are just a click away from imitating the strategy move-by-move, removing the painful process of identifying the best performing currencies and commodities.

The performance of a new investor can increase if he follows an expert.

Investing in stocks is like gambling, but it is not actually gambling. It is a social game. Values can fall as well as rise; you can gain a huge amount of money in a moment and lose it in five minutes. It all depends on your ability to understand and interpret financial analysis and graphs and figure out the perfect moment to invest.

I hope you got the big picture of it now. You don't need to be an expert trader, however, being an expert brings you success in this domain, but you have the possibility to access the trading histories of expert traders and you can learn the entire process from them.

The main idea of social trading is built on four major advantages:

1. Everyone deserves to take advantage of investing in markets without the need for expensive brokerages.

2. Not everyone can monitor real-time market fluctuations because of lack of time.

3. People should have control over what they invest in.

4. Advanced social technology means trading can be democratized and insights easily share globally.

5. You can gain aggregate trading knowledge.

6. You can follow leading traders and make informed market decisions.

Social trading is the best way to access Forex. And you will learn what Forex is and how people make money using this platform.

Forex Trading

Forex, Foreign exchange market, is the most traded financial market in the world.

Every trading day, over 4 trillion dollars' worth of currencies are traded across the globe by banks, institutions, and individual investors.

The trading week for Forex begins Monday morning at 10 A.M. in Sydney, Australia and finishes on Friday evening at 5 P.M. The major financial centers where the currencies are traded are London, New York, Tokyo, Zurich, Frankfurt, Hong Kong, Singapore, Paris, and Sydney.

Unlike other markets you may be familiar with, there is no centralized marketplace for Forex.

Instead, currencies simply trade electronically over-the-counter in whatever major market is open at that time. This means that all the transactions occur via computer networks between traders around the world rather than one centralized exchange.

Currencies play a fundamental role in the world, whether we are aware of it or not, because they need to be exchanged to conduct foreign trade and business.

The need to exchange currencies is the primary objective of the Forex market.

This is why Forex is the largest, most liquid market in the world. It conquers other markets in size, even in stock market, with an average traded value of around U.S. 2000 billion per year.

The key to paving your way to success with currency trading is your ability to speculate on currencies' value. It means that you take a calculated risk to seek a high return over a short time period. It can be a minute, an hour, or a day. It is the opposite of investing, where you have to minimize the risk for a high return over a long period of time like months or years.

The secret is that money can be made here even if the currency is gaining or losing value.

As an example, the Forex traders can sell EUR/USD pairs whenever forecasting the euro to weaken versus the dollar. They can buy USD/EUR if forecasting the dollar to weaken versus the euro.

There are many other markets for trading, but Forex is the largest and the most active one. It also offers tremendous advantages for traders:

- *Free demo account* - This means that Forex brokers offer you the opportunity to learn the strategies and tools for speculation.
- *You can start with small investments* ($200)
- *High liquidity* (Liquidity is the ability of an asset to convert into cash quickly). Market liquidity is the ability

of the market to sell an asset very quickly without being constrained to reduce its price very much.

How to Become Rich from Social Trading

There are three keys for leveraging on Social Trading:

- *Choose an Online Broker*
- *Choose a Social Trading Platform and a Trading Execution Platform*
- *Choose a virtual private server*

1. Choose an Online Broker

A broker is the person who makes the connection between you and the market where you want to trade. He allows your transactions to be in the proper way and timely executed by the institutions that operate on the Forex market.

There are some criteria you should consider when you want to choose an online broker:

- To be regulated because this means protection. They have to respect strict rules that are meant to keep you and the broker safe from fraud.
- When was the Forex broker established? This means that it has to be an old company with prestige and that is trustworthy.
- Trading conditions. Broker companies make money from a percentage of the spreads, or the difference between the buy and the sell prices for each pair of currencies. So the spread has to be variable and low to avoid fraud. If the spread is higher, the broker will earn more money from your trades.

Here is a list with influential brokers:

- *Alpari for UK (http://www.alpari.com)*
- *FXCM Inc. (http://www.fxcm.com)*
- *OANDA Corporation (http://www.oanda.com)*
- *XM (http://xm.com)*

2. Choose a Social Trading Platform and a Trading Execution Platform

Each platform provides possibilities to explore the history of expert traders and gives you information about the profitability and the risk associated with each strategy chosen by traders.

Here are the most well-liked social trading platforms:

- *ZuluTrade* is the most popular social trading platform and it is the one I recommend the most.
- *SimpleTrader*

- *FXJuction*
- *MyFxbook*
- *MQL5*

Each trade made by the trader you have chosen to follow will appear on your broker trading execution platform because it will be synchronized to appear there. Each successful trade will result in a profit in your account and every lost trade as a loss.

3. The Virtual Private Server (VPS)

The Virtual Private Server allows you to be online 24 hours a day to avoid wasted trades, and as a result, money.

You don't have to do this at home. The system works for you 24/7. The VPS will synchronize your trade between the signal provider and the broker with the aim of minimizing the losses in profit.

Social trading really gives those with a minimum amount of money and a limited financial knowledge the opportunity to expand their financial limits and learn how to invest in the stock market using real-time analysis of famous traders.

It is a magnificent opportunity to try to achieve passive income.

On your way, you should remember the golden rule of investment: *"Never invest more than you can't afford to lose."*

Chapter 7: Real Estate Investing

Investing in real estate represents a tremendous opportunity to generate passive income.

It has become increasingly popular over the last decade and it has turned into a common investing machine.

When it comes to real estate, your first thought might be your home, because, for many people, their houses might be the single largest investment they will ever make.

Even if a house is one of the most important investments you will purchase, there are other types of real estate investments that can become a source of wealth.

I would suggest income-producing real estate. It is well known that many high net-worth companies invest in this type of business (life insurance companies, real estate investment trusts, pension funds). But there are also common people who take this path, investing in smaller apartment buildings, duplexes, single family homes, or commodities because they want to achieve a source of passive income through renting them to tenants.

This type of investment is included in the portfolio of investments, next to bonds, stocks, and other securities, but it is quite different from others because real estate is highly tangible, unlike most stocks.

It will bring you a solid feeling of ownership. But its tangibility has also a drawback, because it requires hands-on management.

You need to maintain it. It won't be difficult, but it requires money.

Moreover, when you make that investment, you have to consider the aspects of the real estate because the performance of your properties will impact the performance of your investment.

When you choose to invest in real estate, the first criteria is the location of the property.

But there is another criteria more important than location, which is the type of property – residential homes, shopping malls, warehouses, or office towers.

Every type has a distinct set of drivers that can influence its performance. You can't assume that a type of property will perform in a market where another type is performing amazing. And you can't assume that a type of property will perform successfully now if it has performed well in the past.

When choosing the type of property, there are four big types: offices, retail, industrial, and leased residential.

I have chosen them for a key criteria-income producing.

Houses are also income-producing investments if the afferent cost of the investment can be covered by the rent (mortgages) and if the lender has a rental agreement, this ensures he will receive the monthly payments.

Office Properties

They are the flagship investment for many real estate investors.

Why?

Because of their typical location in the downtown cores and straggling suburban office parks.

The demand for this type of property is very ties to companies' requirements for office workers (on finance, accounting, insurance, real estate, and banks subsidiaries)

If the demand on the labor market grows, the demand for offices grows, too.

The returns for this type of property can be very high. It depends, however, on the market demand, which can be very sensitive to economic performances.

In times of prosperity, offices tend to perform amazingly. They are a very remunerative investment.

Retail property

There is an enormous variety of retail properties, from large shopping malls to single tenant buildings in pedestrian areas.

A conclusive example is Walmart. A retail center has one or more buildings containing smaller tenants.

The demand for this type of property is highly influenced by location, visibility, population density, population growth, and relative income levels.

During the economic growth or retail sales growth, retails tend to perform extraordinarily. Compared to offices, the returns for retails tend to be more stable because retail leases are generally longer and there is a lower tendency for retailers to relocate.

Industrial Property

They are highly regarded as the staple of the average real estate investors because of the minimum requirements they have to satisfy: less management and lower operating costs.

The main factors to consider when investing in industrial properties would be its functionality, location relative to major transport routes, building structure, loading, and the degree of specialization of the place.

Multi-family Residential Property

This type of property delivers the most secure returns because no matter what the economic cycle is, people will always need a place to stay.

On the normal market, the occupancy for residential properties is very high.

Real estate return comes from two parts.

Firstly, the income return comes from the rent payments of tenants.

The second return is the capital return, which is considered when the value of the property increases or decreases as a result of different shifts in the market demand/offer or inflation. It is called appreciation or depreciation of the capital.

Real estate is one of the most common methods that people become wealthy.

Maybe it will not bring you wealth, but it will definitely bring you a long-term source of income.

But you will never know, unless you try.

Chapter 8: Dividend Stock Investing

What is a dividend?

A dividend is a distribution of a portion part of a company's earnings to a class of its shareholders.

It can be in many forms: cash, stocks, or properties. The most stable companies offer to their shareholders dividends.

Even if the price of the dividends doesn't move too much, they are a sign of rewarding, enticing, or retaining investors.

Long-term wealth can be the result of investing in dividend-paying stocks.

Many people invest in dividend-paying stocks to take the advantage of constant payments and the chance to reinvest the dividends to buy additional shares of stocks.

The reason of their investments is that the stock prices of a stable company will always increase over time.

These dividends have low risks, so they represent an appealing investment for people looking for a way to generate safe income long-term and also for those who are waiting for retirement.

The Compound Effect and its Power

This term is used by investors who generate earnings and reinvest the earnings in purchasing additional shares of stock.

This will generate earnings, too, bigger than before.

It serves to illustrate that, in a given time, money can grow, especially if you reinvest it.

The power of compounding has been called *"The eighth wonder of the world"* by Albert Einstein.

With dividend investing, the more often you receive and invest your dividends, the higher the rate of return.

To take advantage of the power of compounding your investments, you need an initial investment, earnings from dividends or interests, reinvestment of your earnings, and time to fructify your investment.

Dividend Reinvestment Plan-DRIP

DRIP is an ideal way to increase the value of your investment.

If you need a plan for reinvesting, a DRIP is what you need. DRIP is the name of the dividend reinvesting plan offered by companies that allows investors to automatically reinvest cash dividends in buying shares on the dividend payment date. This will facilitate the compounding potential of your investment.

It is very attractive for companies because the DRIP shares can be sold directly by companies, without the necessity of exchange and the money can be reinvested in the company. There is a major disadvantage for investors or shareholders: they must pay the taxes on cash dividends reinvested even if they have never received cash.

In conclusion, investing in dividend-paying stocks is a valuable source of passive income.

Today, you have the tools and strategies to make informed decisions and decide what investment fits perfectly with your investing style, time horizon, financial situation, and short- and long-term objectives.

The main idea is to take action. Everything you will achieve in life will be the result of acting toward a dream, an idea, a vision, or a passion.

I just remembered something*... "There was an old story about a man who* *prayed to God that he would win the lottery.*

Every night, he got down on his knees and pleaded with the Almighty to hit the jackpot. After a month, he looked to the heavens and wondered why God still hadn't granted his prayer. He heard a loud booming voice come from above that simply said, 'At the very least, you could have bought a ticket!'"

The message of the story is simple. If you want to achieve something in life, it is not enough to pray for it, you have to take action. Don't lose your time dreaming unless you are willing to sacrifice something to achieve it.

Dreams without action are worthless.

So, if you consider investing a solution for becoming rich, find out your investment strategy and take action.

I would suggest you invest in Apple stocks because the stock recently split and now sells for $133, the price being more accessible now for individual investors. The price of a stock decreased from $700 and now is the perfect time to add it in your portfolio of investments.

I know that investing in stocks is a risky way of generating passive income, but as I told you, stable companies will always increase the dividend price, year after year, because they want to retain, entice, and reward their investors.

They are companies with prestige and financial stability. However, nothing is guaranteed and if you decide to buy a stock, you should understand that it may go down.

Chapter 9: Bond Ladders or Bond Interest

If you find stocks too risky for you, bond interests represent the perfect solution for achieving financial freedom, taking the slightest risk of losing the money invested.

There are a lot of people who think so, and technically, they are correct. If you compare the index funds of stocks and bonds, you will find that bonds have much more secure returns.

What is a bond?

A bond is a payment of a debt where you collect the interest for being a lender.

You loan your money to a company, a city, a government, and they promise to pay you back in full, with regular interest payments.

They are used to raise money and finance a variety of projects and activities. If you decide to invest your money in bonds, you will become a debt holder/creditor or issuer.

The Mechanism Behind Bonds:

The mechanism is simple. When companies or entities need to get more money to finance their projects, refinance existing debts, or maintain some operations that are ongoing in that moment, they will issue bonds to investors instead of getting loans from banks. The issuer of the bond will sign a contract with the investor, setting the interest rate-coupon that will be paid when the loan has to be returned.

The price of the issued bond depends on the set of factors that includes the credit quality of the issuer, the length of time until the expiration of the loan, the interest rate (coupon) that is compared to the general interest rate settled on the market in that moment.

When the bond's term expires, you receive the money back from your loan.

Then you can reinvest them in bonds and receive even more interest as income.

Chapter 10: CD Ladders

They are similar to the Bond Ladders, but the difference stands in the low level of risk.

What is a CD ladder?

A CD ladder is a strategy in which an investor divides the amount of money to be invested into equal amounts to certificates of deposit (CDs) with different maturity dates.

This strategy decreases both interest rate and re-investment risks.

In your portfolio of investments with periodic cash you will find different CDs with different maturity dates.

For CDs, the payment is periodically established as opposed to normal bonds with the interest paid at maturity date.

For CDs, the payment is periodically established as opposed to normal bonds with the interest paid at maturity date.

Another difference is that CD ladders are fully taxable and they are available only through banks and they have FDIC insurance (Federal Deposit Insurance Corporation).

In the financial world, CD ladders are one of the safest methods of investing your money and getting cash flow quarterly.

This is an example of CD ladders portfolio, which is spread on 5 years. What you can see there is called **diversification** of the maturity dates. In this way, the investor will always get cash flow and he will invest it in more CD ladders.

Chapter 11: Affiliate Marketing

Affiliate Marketing has become one of the top business opportunities online because the startup costs are very low and the income it can generate is overwhelmingly impressive.

The Concept

Affiliate Marketing is the strategy that involves creating your own website or blog and sending your traffic to someone else's blog to buy their products or services.

For every sale initiated by a link from your site, you will earn a commission — an *affiliate sales commission*.

You can start this business in few hours but your success is based on the amount of time and effort you devote to it.

What is the Mechanism?

1. Create a website or a blog. To start a business as an affiliate marketer, you have to create a website where you will place the links of the products and services you want to recommend to your visitors.

2. Decide your product/service niche

Choose a topic you are familiar with or one you are excited to learn about.

3. Find products or services to promote

Many affiliate platforms have the purpose to connect customers with affiliate site publishers who can help with selling their products/services.

- *ClickBank, E-junkey, PayDotCom* help connect eBook writers and software creators with affiliates to help them sell their digital products.
- *Google AdSense* doesn't require your work and involvement to result in a sale. Your income is achieved by leading your traffic to a trader site.

4. Affiliate site content

Here are two approaches of creating an affiliate marketing site:

- **Resource sites** that are focused on providing different articles about how to do something, then recommending affiliate links and banners.
- **Review sites**. Here you have to review those items/products and influence the decision of your website visitors on buying a product. For each product you review, you have to place a link or a banner ad that clicks through for sale on your merchant site.

5. Affiliate sites have to attract a lot of targeted traffic to succeed:

To attract potential customers, you have to bring traffic to your site (highly targeted traffic).

There are four strategies to bring potential customers:

-*Paid advertising*, where you can use Google AdSense.

-*Free Advertising Sites* like Craigslist and US Free Ads.

-*Article Marketing* - This is a very popular method for marketing your affiliate site that provides a lot of benefits. You will build reliability and credibility as a source for information in your niche. This will help to increase your search engine ranking because it's increasing the amount of links that point to your site. With an increase in your links, you will bring more traffic to your site.

-*E-mail Marketing* - Capturing the names of your engaged visitors and email addresses and sending them e-mail with different products or services.

The fundamental aspect in getting money from affiliate marketing is to love what you do and work constantly to improve the quality of your website. In this way, you will work for passion, not for necessity.

Steve Jobs said, *"The only way to do great work is to love what you do. If you haven't found it yet, keep looking. Don't settle."*

Chapter 12. Another Gold Mine - Annuities

Annuities have an interesting, compelling, and fascinating history.

You may not even imagine when the concept started.

Although they have only existed in this formula for a few decades, the idea of paying an amount of income to an individual or a family dates back to the Roman Empire.

The old formula used the Latin word *annua* with the meaning of an annual stipend and during the reign of emperors, the word was used to describe a contract that made annual payments.

It is said that the earliest dealer of annuities in the history is the Roman speculator and jurist, Gnaeus Domitius Annius Ulpianis, who is also known for creating the actuarial life table, which is a table or spreadsheet that reflects the probability of a person at a certain age dying before their next birthday. This system is based on statistical calculations, considering statistic indicators such as the mortality rate or gender.

In ancient Rome, Roman soldiers were paid with annuities for their military services.

During the Middle Ages, lords and kings used annuities as a monetary source for covering the war or conflicts' expenses.

And they continued to have the same direction.

In 1759, annuities reached America in the form of a retirement pool for church pastors in Pennsylvania.

In the 1930s, annuities were just a small piece of the U.S. insurance market, but the perspective changed because of two factors. It was development that drove the term "annuity" to expansion.

One of the major concerns of investors during the Great Depression was to find a secure, stable way of investing their money.

They oriented their perspective on the products offered by insurance companies because they were perceived as stable institutions.

They were flexible, payment deferred annuities, which allowed investors to save and accumulate assets as well as draw down principal.

The second development is represented by the growth of the group annuity market for corporate pensions, which began its expansion in 1930s.

What is an annuity?

An annuity is a contractual financial product sold by financial companies (banks, trust companies, insurance companies, or investment dealers) that is created to accept and grow funds from an individual and then upon annuitization, pay out a stream of payments to the individual at a later point in time.

The period of time when an annuity is being funded and before payouts begin is referred to as the accumulation phase.

In this period, money is invested.

Once payments start, the contract is in the annuitization phase (the period when the annuitant, the person who receives the benefits of an annuity, starts to receive the payments).

Phases of the Annuity Contract

The contract of annuities is represented by three phases: accumulation, annuitization, and payout.

Accumulation phase - It is the first phase in the life of any annuity contract and it starts after the initial payment is made. It will last until the payments are scheduled to begin from the contract.

There are three fundamental categories of annuities:

1. Fixed annuities are a type of contract that guarantees both the investor's principal plus a fixed rate of interest. They have the same mechanism as the Certificates of Deposit, with the exception that they grow tax-deferred.

Being the oldest type from the annuities category, fixed annuities are among the safest investments available.

One of the main benefits of fixed annuities is the high rate of interest they pay. They tend to be slightly higher than CDs, treasuries, or savings bonds.

 The reason is because insurance carriers invest the assets of their clients into a portfolio of long-term bonds and assume all of the naked risk from them, passing the majority of the earnings on to the contract holders.

2. Indexed annuities are the newest debutant in the insurance market. They are similar with fixed annuities because they guarantee the principal and a set term, but they don't pay the fixed rate.

Money is invested in one of the major stock market indices. The contract owner gets a share of the market' growth, if there it is one, avoiding any downside risk.

The reason contract owners are protected by any risk is because companies use different methods to credit their contract holders with market gains.

We can define two significant methods:

- **Annual reset**- The annuitant is credited with a return each year that the market exceeds its previous year's level. If it doesn't, then no gain is credited, but no loss is considered either.
- **Point to point** - They measure the evolution in the index from the start of the contract to the end of the

term. In the continuous bull market, the higher returns are ordinary.

3. *Variable annuities* are the most complex annuities from the market. In fact, they are the most complex elements from the investing portfolio.

The value of your investment as a variable annuity owner will vary depending on the performance of the investment options you choose.

The investment options for a variable annuity are typically mutual funds that invest in stocks, bonds, money market instruments, or some combination of the three.
Variable annuities let you receive periodic payments for the rest of your life. This offers protection against the possibility that, after you retire, you will outlive your assets.

They have also a death benefit. If you die before the insurer has started making payments to you, your beneficiary is guaranteed to receive a specified amount – typically, at least the amount of your purchase payments.

Your beneficiary will get a benefit from this feature if, at the time of your death, your account value is less than the guaranteed amount.

They are also tax-deferred. That means you pay no taxes on the income and investment gains from your annuity until you withdraw your money.

You may also transfer your money from one investment option to another within a variable annuity without paying tax at the time of the transfer.

When cashing your money out of a variable annuity, however, you will be taxed on the earnings at ordinary income tax rates rather than lower capital gains rates.

In general, the benefits of tax deferral will outweigh the costs of a variable annuity only if you hold it as a long-term investment to meet retirement and other long-range goals.

Variable annuities are designed to meet the expectations of long-term goals or retirement, not short-term goals because many insurance companies may charge if you withdraw money early. They also involve investment risks.

Are annuities an efficient investment?

It depends on your needs and the type of annuity you choose.

They are a lump sum of cash invested to produce a monthly stream of income for a fixed period or lifetime.

The income can be set to start now, immediate annuities, or in a certain time in the future, deferred annuities.

This is why you should be really informed when you choose one of the types as a possible investment, with the aim of generating passive income over time.

Conclusion

If you want to be absolutely free, the first thing you should do is to change the way you live your life.

"If you want something you have never had, then you have got to do something you have never done."

Think about what makes you happy!

Dig into your mind for the perfect and honest answer.

Your passions may turn into valuable sources of passive income.

Now that you have discovered tremendous opportunities to change your financial position, the next step should be *planning,* then *action*.

Make a start and create your future! Rewrite the rules of work and work from home for your dreams.

Become successful!

Be happy!

In the end, thank you for purchasing this book.

If you have a moment, please leave me an honest review. I am constantly focused on accumulating more knowledge and improving my performance.